Trekking to Mustang, 1964

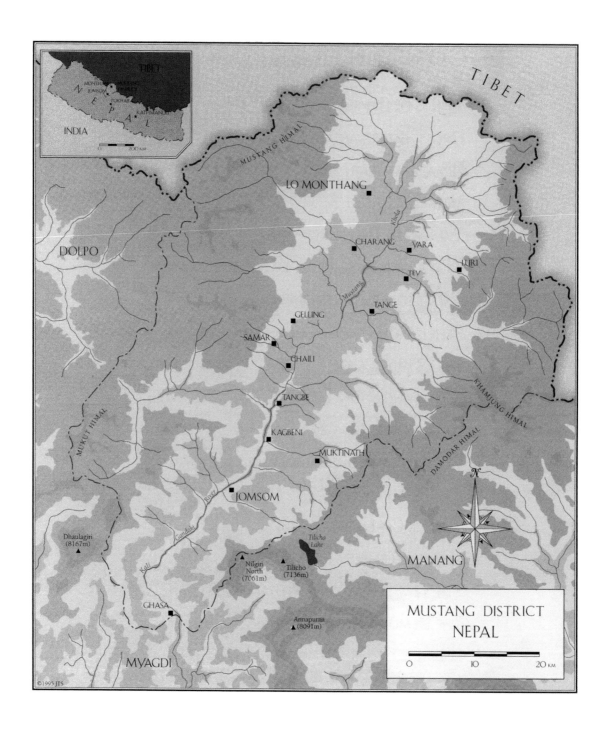

TIBET

MUSTANG HIMAL

LO MONTHANG

DOLPO

CHARANG
VARA
TUR
TEV
TANGE

GELLING

SAMAR
GHAILI

TANGBE

KAGBENI
MUKTINATH

KHAMJUNG HIMAL

MUKUT HIMAL

DAMODAR HIMAL

JOMSOM

MANANG

Dhaulagiri
(8167m)

Nilgiri
North
(7061m)
Tilicho
(7136m)

Tilicho
Lake

GHASA

Annapurna
(8091m)

MYAGDI

MUSTANG DISTRICT
NEPAL

0   10   20 KM

©1995 JTS

TIBET

NEPAL

INDIA

0   200 KM

Trekking to Mustang, 1964

Crossing Paths with Mastiffs and Khampas in the Himalayan Kingdom of Lo

by

David Rosenberg

Trekking to Mustang, 1964
Crossing Paths with Mastiffs and Khampas in the Himalayan Kingdom of Lo

First Edition, September 2016

Interior and cover design by Winslow Colwell/Wren Song Design

Published in the United States by Wren Song Press
PO Box 6, East Middlebury, Vermont 05740

map pg. iii: Source: Peter Matthiessen, *East of Lo Monthang: In the Land of Mustang*. Boston, Shambhala, 1995.
photo, pg. v: Chorten Buddhist shrine, near Tsarang.

The text of this publication was set in Myriad.

ISBN: 978-0-9753706-4-3

Acknowledgements

I am deeply indebted to Stu Ullmann for his chronological trail notes and photos as well as to Tony Drexler for all his insights and anecdotes of our trek. Without their contributions, this story could not have been written. The narrative has greatly benefited from the skillful editing of Don Messerschmidt (EditWithUs.com), Deborah Faeyrglenn, Erica Fisher, Jack Mayer, and — above all — my first, last, and most kind and encouraging editor, Jean Rosenberg.

PROLOGUE

We had the experience but missed the meaning,

And approach to the meaning restores the experience

In a different form, beyond any meaning

We can assign to happiness. I have said before

That the past experience revived in the meaning

Is not the experience of one life only

But of many generations — not forgetting

Something that is probably quite ineffable.

— TS Eliot, *The Dry Salvages*, 1941

Trekking up the Kali Gandaki to "the roof of the world."

INTRODUCTION

This is an account of a remarkable journey that Tony Drexler, Stu Ullmann, and I took over fifty years ago when we were Peace Corps Volunteers in Nepal. I am writing this narrative of our adventures to reassure ourselves it actually happened and to share this extraordinary adventure with our families and friends.

Over the course of three and a half weeks in September and October of 1964, we crossed the Himalayas on foot, climbing in and out of the deepest and steepest river gorge on earth, to the remote Mustang District of Nepal which encompasses the ancient Kingdom of Lo and its walled capital of Lo Manthang. Our journey would take us from the terraced rice paddies around the hill villages of central Nepal, to coniferous forests on the steep southern slopes of the Himalayas, and then across the passes between the high peaks to the arid, wind-eroded Tibetan Plateau.

We had heard stories about this distant, ancient Buddhist kingdom on the northern slopes of the Himalayas. It was a very remote, walled town, with ancient temples, a palace, a siege fortress, and a caravansary. We were familiar with the Tibetan caravans of pack animals that had travelled from Tibet across the Himalayas through the deep gorges along the Kali Gandaki to the central market bazaar in Pokhara, and then on to India. The pack mules and ponies usually wore headdresses and harnesses with bells attached. We could hear the bells echoing through the hills and gorges in the hills around Pokhara.

This was an awesome adventure, culturally and spiritually. The area we and many Nepalis call Mustang was once the independent Kingdom of Lo or the town of Lo Manthang, in Tibetan. It was founded in 1380 by Ame Pal, the Tibetan warrior. He directed the construction of the town walls of Lo Manthang and many of its still-standing structures. The neighboring areas were mostly settled by Tibetan and Thakali ethnic groups in several scattered villages. Tibetan Buddhist culture, religion, and tradition had been better preserved in this region than almost anywhere else in the world.

Along the way, we inadvertently crossed paths with a group of Khampas. These were anti-Chinese resistance fighters from the eastern Tibetan region of Kham who had set up base camps around Mustang District. It was a good place for them, a remote location with no clear boundaries and ambiguous sovereignty, right on the Nepal-China border. The Kingdom of Lo had a semi-autonomous status recognized in the Nepali government constitution. At the time of our trek in 1964, the Nepal-China border had not been officially delineated. As we trekked across the Himalayas, we became increasingly aware and alarmed about the clashes between Khampas and Chinese forces in the area. Perhaps this was not a good time for us to get a Nepal government trekking permit to Mustang. We never asked for one. Our journey subsequently led to a minor but highly regrettable Cold War incident.

We had come to Nepal in September 1963 as part of a group of 40 Peace Corps Volunteers to work on rural community development projects for the Panchayat (or local council) Development Ministry. David and Stu were assigned to work with a multi-purpose team of Nepali counterparts in the Pokhara valley. Tony was assigned in the adjacent district of Syangja.

. . . .

Our trek to Mustang had its origins in an unexpected encounter that David and Stu had with a small and exhausted group of impoverished Tibetans who had stopped to rest in a field near our home in Pokhara in late 1963. They were a small fragment of the many Tibetans who left their homeland in eastern Tibet in 1959 with the Dalai Lama and thousands of his followers. They were fleeing from Chinese military forces who were strengthening their control over Tibetan society. These refugees had walked across the Himalayas and across much of northern India and Nepal for several years, looking for sanctuaries in exile.

Our Nepali neighbors weren't sure where this particular group of Tibetan refugees had come from, where they were going, or how long they would be staying. We were able to help them set up camp on a piece of idle land nearby in Hyangja, a small village northwest of the Pokhara bazaar. We thought it would be a suitable, temporary resting place for them.

In our efforts to help these Tibetan refugees, we sought help from local and international aid workers, including the Nepal Red Cross and a Swiss aid agency working in the area. We also contacted Tibetans we knew around Pokhara, in particular, Amdo Kesang, proprietor of the Tibet Restaurant and Guest Lodge at the Pokhara airport.

Tibetan pack train of mules and ponies loading up on the main trail through the Pokhara bazaar. The caravan is coming south from Mustang, along the Thak Khola and Kali Gandaki rivers.

It was at Amdo Kesang's restaurant that David later met Tsewang Palbar, the younger son of the King of Mustang. He was going from Mustang to Dharamsala to meet with the Dalai Lama. He thanked David for his help in setting up the refugee camp and invited him and Stu to visit him and his family in Mustang. We asked Tony to join us on this trek. The three of us would take our vacation during the upcoming Nepali holiday of Dasain. During this 15-day autumn holiday celebrating an ancient mythic battle among Hindu deities, government and business offices are closed. Religious processions are held in many communities. Families gather for special ceremonies and feasts. And we would trek across the Himalayas.

Mustang is more accurately known as Lo Manthang, the main town of the traditional Kingdom of Lo or the Mustang District of Nepal. It is located at the top of the watershed of the Kali Gandaki River, north of the Himalayas. Over many millennia, the river has carved its way from the Tibetan Plateau through the Himalayas, between the Annapurna and Dhaulagiri mountain ranges. These mountain peaks are over three miles higher than the river valley between them. The slope from the riverside village of Kokhethanti to the top of Dhaulagiri is about 49%. The Kali Gandaki flows south through Nepal to India and into the Ganges River and the Bay of Bengal. For centuries, it has been a pilgrimage route for Hindus to the home of the gods.

Due to its remote frontier location, Mustang has always had a high degree of autonomy. But its strategic location along a major caravan route through the Himalayas also ensured a small but steady flow of traditional commerce. There has been a caravan trade along this route across the Himalayas for centuries. Ponies, mules, donkeys, and yaks were used as pack animals to carry salt, wool, and gems to the south and brought back rice and manufactured goods to the north. Sheep, goats, and yaks were the main pastoral animals in Mustang, providing milk, meat, and hides. Horses were the fastest means of transport for people. Almost all horses in Mustang belonged to the King's family and the few people prosperous enough to afford them.

We had been invited to visit the Kingdom of Mustang in the autumn of 1964, long before Mustang was open to tourists, before the border between Nepal and Tibet was clearly defined, before there were any roads, cars, electricity, or indoor plumbing in this remote area. We had a rough idea of where to go but no idea of where to find food and lodging. Fortunately, Amdo Kesang showed us the route and gave us several letters of introduction to the headmen of villages on the north side of the Himalayas where we could stop for food, shelter, and rest. The envelopes were thick; apparently they contained more than a letter of introduction. Each was addressed in Tibetan. David wrote the English transliteration for each village name. We didn't think much more about it. It might have been wishful thinking, but we thought these "letters of safe conduct" would be sufficient for our journey.

The first group of refugees squatted on rice paddies near our house and the Panchayat Development Office.

Amdo Kesang (at the left) and his family with Peace Corps Director Sargent Shriver.

Tibetan refugees hand-carding and spinning wool in Hyangja. This later became the Tashi Palkhiel Tibetan Settlement.

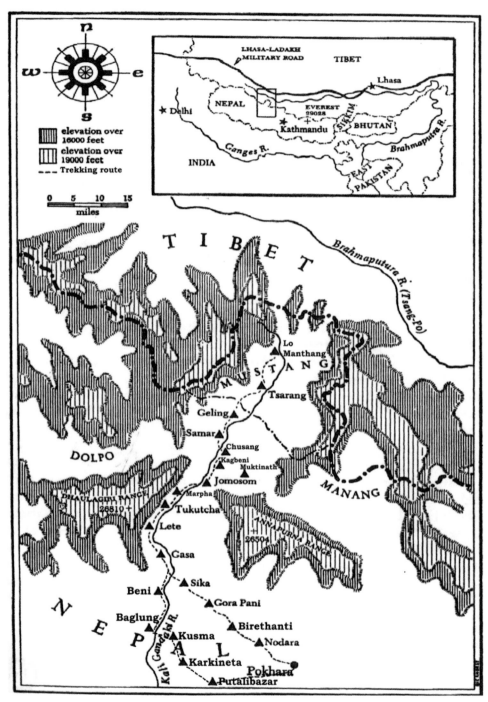

Base map from Michel Peissel,
Mustang: A Lost Tibetan Kingdom,
Delhi: Book Faith India, 1967

PART 1

Ascending the Kali Gandaki Gorge through the Himalayas

The story that follows uses the place names we were familiar with at the time. Many of them are known by other names, not surprising given the numerous languages and dialects spoken along our route. The photos show the dramatic changes in the landscape as we travelled from south to north. We started from Pokhara Valley, where the lowest point at the lake, Phewa Tal, is 2713 feet or 827 meters above sea level. The highest point we reached was Nyi-La Pass, into Mustang District, about 13000 feet or 4000 meters. The ups and downs seemed endless.

September 19

Our journey began with an easy 14-mile walk from Pokhara to Putalibazar, where Tony was stationed. We climbed out of Pokhara valley, over the pass at the small village of Nawakot, and waded through a few shallow rocky streams on the way to Putalibazar. The three of us spent the next day getting ready to head north. We would travel as light as possible with only our Peace Corps-issued backpacks, some clothes, our sleeping bags, and a first-aid kit. No porters, no Sherpas.

September 21

We left Putalibazar early in the morning and started north, zig-zagging up the river valley. Thatch roof and mud wall houses were scattered around rice paddies and vegetable plots along the trail. We had our midday meal at a bhatti, a trailside teahouse run by a Thakali family. The Thakali people are a Tibetan Buddhist ethnic group in the Thak Khola region around the Mustang District. Thakalis are well-known as middlemen and merchants who serve the caravan trade and, more recently, the tourist trade. This bhatti in the village of Chilauni Bas was run by Utar Kumari, daughter of the prominent Tulachan family in Tukche. We arrived in Karkineta about 5 P.M., and stayed at Narandata Sharma's house. So far, so good.

September 22

After departing Karkineta, we crossed the bridges over the Modi Khola and Kali Gandaki about noon. Crossing bridges in the Himalayas can be quite exciting. These bridges were foot bridges supported by twisted iron cables first put up by Scottish engineers with the British Gurkha regiments over a hundred years ago.

We went up the west side of the Kali Gandaki, and got to Baglung about 5:00 P.M. We stayed at a Thakali bhatti near the Panchayat office. It served good dal-bhat, (lentils and rice) but the raksi (a home-brewed, alcoholic drink distilled from rice or millet) was only mediocre. However, it put us to sleep fast.

September 23

From Baglung, we trekked on to Beni by mid-morning for dal-bhat. We then had to cross the Myagdi Khola which joins the Kali Gandaki here. Unfortunately, the foot bridge was unfinished. There were four suspension cables across the river, but no side wires connecting the top and bottom cables and no planks to walk on. We had a choice. We could go out of our way a few miles upstream and cross at another point. Or we could cross the rushing river by grasping the upper cable and shuffling along the lower cable. At this early stage in our journey, we felt strong and confident enough to take the grasp-and-shuffle approach. One at a time, we went. However, the cables soon became too slack to both grasp above and shuffle on below. We had to finish the crossing by going hand over hand to reach the other side, with a full pack on our backs. It was more exciting than we anticipated. It should have been a forewarning about unanticipated events ahead. On we went to Rakhu by mid-afternoon and Beg Khola for the night.

September 24

We left Beg Khola early, surrounded by mist and fog, and had our dal-bhat mid-morning at Tatopani (named after the hot springs along the river). The trail then went through a mountain rain forest and was quite narrow. In many places, it was carved out of a steep hill with mossy rocks and big ferns on one side and the river with roaring rapids surging around big boulders on the other side. It was intensely green and lush. We passed through Dana by midafternoon, and arrived in Ghasa before dark for food and sleep. Bordered by pastures of lush grass, the village has long been a caravan stop for horses and other grazing livestock. Fortunately, there was a room for us.

David and Tony on the trail above the Kali Gandaki, between Kusma and Baglung

We washed whenever and wherever we could. That wasn't often.

Tony crossing Myagdi Khola, starting the hand-over-hand part.

Tony and David in fern gully.

September 25

There was a steady light rain as we left Ghasa early. The higher we went, the wetter it got as we trekked through the mist. In any weather, the Thak Khola valley has some spectacular geology. Near Lete, we came across one high hill shrouded in a dense rain cloud. Waterfalls were flowing down from it and around moss-covered boulders to a flowering poppy field.

By mid-morning, we had dal-bhat in Lete. This part of the journey had fairly level walking, through small clusters of houses along the Kali Gandaki, as the riverbed slowly widened out. We went through Devitan, Larjung, and Sokung, into the heart of Thakali country, and arrived in Tukche in the late afternoon, tired and ready for food and sleep.

It had recently rained in Tukche. The narrow path through the village was muddy. The white-walled houses lining the path were also mud-splattered. In an open space between the houses there was a small temple or shrine. Beyond that was a house with a white door frame and lintel and a dark-colored door. This was to be our guest house for the night. The entrance room had whitewashed walls, a chulo (cooking hearth) in the corner, and woven grass mats with small Tibetan carpets on the floor.

New bridge at Devitan, with prayer flags. Beyond it, on the right, is the village gompa.

Waterfall and poppy field near Lete.

Trekking past Khanti, between Devitan and Tukche.

Main street in Tukche.

September 26

We had a restful morning in Tukche, and left for Jomsom about noon. The landscape changed quickly and dramatically here. We walked along one side of the wide stony riverbed of the Kali Gandaki. Immense, barren steep ridges were on both sides. Vegetation and growth became sparse on the valley floor. We could see the Dhaulagiri Himal (literally, "great white peaks") to the southwest and the Nilgiris ("great blue peaks") to the east. The Nilgiris blocked our view of the western and northern sides of the Annapurna Range.

The trail took us through the beautiful Thakali town of Marpha. Lining the narrow lane through the town were several well-built, two story stone houses with finely carved balcony windows. The lane also had stone and slate-lined gutters and culverts. The houses had flat roofs with stacks of wood for fuel around the perimeter. The roofs were also used for drying dung for fuel. Most of the houses had square interior courtyards. It was a place to milk their cows, yaks, or goats. In some courtyards, there was a mulch pit in the center for dung and evergreen branches. We had Tibetan tea (called po cha or suja, very strong black tea, with lots of yak butter and salt in it) and momos (fried dumplings filled with goat meat) at a very well-stocked store. It had biscuits, batteries, cigarettes, basmati rice, apples, and even apricots. The prices were as high as the altitude.

Later that afternoon, we arrived at the Nepali government military checkpoint outside Jomsom. Back in 1964, this was the effective northern limit of Nepal's domestic sovereignty. To the north was the autonomous Kingdom of Mustang and the walled city of Lo Manthang. That's where we wanted to go. There was also a branch trail to the east to the Hindu temple at Muktinath, a popular pilgrimage destination for Hindu and Buddhist Nepalis and Indians. In Sanskrit, "mukti" means salvation and "nath" means god. The main pagoda temple there is dedicated to the god Vishnu, the Lord of Salvation. For Tibetan Buddhists, Muktinath is an important place of Dakinis, goddesses known as Sky Dancers.

Jomsom is located at a critical cultural and geographic crossroad. It has a Nepal Army outpost. It is on the Hindu and Buddhist pilgrim route to Muktinath. It is the gateway to the Tibetan Plateau. It marks the boundary between the land of rice and millet eaters and the land of tsampa and barley eaters. The most adept intermediaries of these different worlds are Thakali traders. For many generations, they have exchanged salt from the salt lakes of Western Tibet for rice from the hills of Nepal.

We were reassured to find that we were acquainted with the Nepali army officer stationed there, Major Rana. We had a letter of introduction for him from his counterpart in Pokhara. The letter asked permission for us to proceed north to Mustang. Major Rana was friendly and polite, but said we would now need a special pass from Kathmandu, because fifteen days earlier four Nepalis had been shot somewhere nearby on the Nepal side of the border. This was a shocking surprise to us. We knew the borders were unclear if not contested. But we didn't know people were getting killed. Who exactly were killed, Nepalis? Khampas?

Others? Who killed them? Where? And why?

Despite this alarming news, we clung to our letters of introduction as our assurance of safe passage. We urged Major Rana to let us proceed, based on our letters and on our promise that we were not going to go anywhere near the border. We said we only wanted to go as far as Lo Manthang to visit the King, whose son had invited us to visit him there.

According to Major Rana and the local police commissioner, there were only a few, very small Nepali military units along the China border. In addition, there were a few border posts with Nepali police and some others with Indian military observers. The police commissioner told us the military at the border posts were very ill-equipped. He also told us there were some Khampa guerrilla camps in the Mustang region. He said the Nepali Army could only visit these camps with advance permission from the Khampas. Certain parts of the camps were off limits to them. He told us the Khampas had new automatic weapons and an unknown quantity of ammunition.

After a lengthy discussion, Major Rana finally told us that if we proceeded to trek north from Kagbeni, it would be solely our responsibility. If we had any kind of trouble, he could not give us official permission of any kind.

What to do? We stayed in Jomsom that night to think it over.

Thakali mule train in Marpha with baskets of dung for compost and fuel. Gutters for runoff and sewage were bridged with stones and timbers. Roofs are stacked with fuel wood.

Tibetan Khampas resting in front of a teahouse in Jomsom.

September 27

We decided to go to Muktinath for the morning. But instead of returning all the way back to Jomsom, we would stop over at Kagbeni. It's a town about halfway back from Muktinath where the Jhong Khola meets the Kali Gandaki. We said goodbye to Major Rana in Jomsom and told him we were going to visit the holy pilgrimage site of Muktinath, and then return to stay in Kagbeni. From there, we would head north the next day. But we didn't tell that part to Major Rana.

Since we were already in Mustang District, we assumed we would have no problem trekking through the district all the way up to the walled town of Lo Manthang. Once we got there, we thought that — even without a Nepali government permit — we could talk to the checkpoint guards outside the town gate and show them our letter of introduction to the King of Mustang. We hoped that would get us into the town to see some of its famous temples and tangkas. Then we could return the way we came. That was our plan. In retrospect, it was a naïve plan, with too much wishful thinking in it. Things didn't turn out the way we had expected.

We went through Khingar and Jharkot, ascending from 9,000 to 10,000 feet elevation, and passing many chortens, gompas, and mani walls along the way. Chortens are Buddhist monuments, often commemorating a lama. Gompas are Buddhist temples or monasteries. Mani walls are stone plates or rocks carved with prayers from Buddhist scriptures.

All are widely seen in Tibetan areas. We were always careful to pass them on the left, Buddhist style. In the chortens on this trail, we could see shaligrams or rocks with fossils of shells embedded in them. Many eons ago, they may have been on the riverbed or seabed of a tectonic plate that was pushed up to the surface by the still-growing Himalayan mountains. It was a graphic reminder that the Kali Gandaki was older than the Himalayas.

We arrived in Muktinath, 12,336 feet above sea level, late in the afternoon. We found the temple, but daylight was starting to fade, so we started looking for lodging. We met a man who knew a place for us to stay. We went with him down to the town, across some fields and through the small settlement of Purang.

Characteristically, there was one level path through lined by about a dozen Tibetan style houses, with white walls, flat roofs, and ladders leading up to the roofs. At the end of these, there was a small inn where we could stay for the night. It was a pretty place, but the food was not very good dal-bhat. We also had some chirpi, rock-hard and tasteless cheese. By now, we were used to chewing it very slowly and carefully, being careful not to break a tooth. We were hungry enough to eat almost anything.

A family from Manang on the trail from Jomsom to Jharkot. The hunchbacked man limped
slowly, but they had all made it over Thorung La Pass, altitude 5416 Meters or 17,769 feet.

Jharkot, with irrigated fields below.

A dharamsala or resting place for pilgrims at Rani Pauwa near Muktinath.

Muktinath Shrine with water-powered prayer wheel.

A Hindu Sadhu pilgrim, Tony, our host in Purang, and David talking in Muktinath.

Tony and our host discuss the price of food for dinner. In Muktinath, it was 5 rupees, about twice the cost in Pokhara. Tony appears incredulous. But we had no alternatives.

September 28

In the morning, we got up early and went back to the temple at Muktinath. We saw the eternal fire — actually, a few flickering flames — next to a rivulet flowing out of a rock cave. Next to it was a flat stone-lined washing area with three pilgrims bathing under spouts of very cold water. The water spouts were shaped like carved bull heads. There was a water wheel in a small stream turning a prayer wheel. It was a perpetual motion prayer wheel. We wandered around the temples and rest houses. Eventually, we went on our way towards Kagbeni. On our return through Purang, we had a morning meal of potatoes roasted in the coals of the kitchen hearth at the house where we had slept the night before.

As we slowly trekked down the trail high above the Jhong Khola, we had stunning panoramic views of high mountain peaks and ridges encompassing a vast barren landscape of a brown-gray valley with contrasting small patches of brilliant green irrigated fields.

We arrived at Kagbeni just before dark. There was a wild and strange feel to this town. The men were quite tall and looked very strong. They all had long black hair, high Tibetan boots, and were armed with daggers in silver-colored sheaths. They must be Khampas, we thought. Many of the women wore multi-colored garb with reds, greens, and yellows woven into a black background. Only a few spoke Nepali. Those that did, just spoke a little of it.

This change of culture and people had begun just north of Tukche. But Kagbeni was very different from anything we had known in Nepal south of the Himalayas. The landscape was filled with spectacular natural beauty, combining high snow peaks with small, verdant cultivated fields. Few and far between were small settlements in a vast high plateau of barren valleys and hills. We ambled down the trail between Jharkot and Purang in late afternoon sunlight, through attractive fields of wheat, barley, buckwheat, and root crops.

On our way into Kagbeni, as it was getting dark, cloudy, and windy, we came across a very large funeral procession. We were barely able to figure out what had happened. The funeral ritual was for a man who had died about three days ago. Right after he died, his family threw his body into the Kali Gandaki. The procession was led by about 40 Lamas who were reclaiming the dead man's soul and releasing it from some kind of purgatory. Lamas were playing horns and trumpets, beating cymbals and drums, or chanting prayers. The lamas were followed by about 30 family members and relatives, and other wailing mourners.

Near the front of the procession, there was an effigy of the dead man seated on a horse. It was held up by a family member who was seated on a horse behind the effigy. A brightly colored umbrella was held and twirled over the dummy's head as the procession slowly wove its way through the streets of Kagbeni, down to the Kali Gandaki. The effigy was dismembered and tossed into the river along with a small flaming pot, freeing the dead man's soul and spirit. The wailing of mourners and the sorrowful sound of horns, drums, and cymbals slowly tapered off.

Somehow, we made our way in darkness to our lodging for the night. After a meal of Tibetan flatbread, potatoes and yak cheese, we climbed a ladder into an upper room where mats and rugs had been laid out for us. We slept fitfully.

Purang house backyard with woman spreading dung to dry for fuel. We stayed in the room on the right.

Kids in Jharkot grinding grain with stone mortar and pestle, next to shrine with prayer wheels.

Below Jharkot, women harvesting grain.

In Kagbeni, the kids were as curious about us as we were about them.

Funeral procession in Kagbeni with clothed effigy of the deceased on horseback.

September 29

In the morning, we could see that the house we were staying in was quite large. It was two stories high and built around a wide square interior courtyard. We took our meals on the ground floor around the chulo in the main room. There was a small window looking into the courtyard where we saw two men packing up a mule. They were large men, over 6 feet, with broad shoulders, long unwashed dark hair, and long robes. We thought they were Khampas, getting ready to head north.

Our day started early with cold and gusty winds. We all were somewhat apprehensive, heading into unknown territory in more ways than one. But once we started out, we had a surge of exhilaration. We were determined to see as much as possible of this remote valley kingdom, tucked between Nepal and the Tibetan plateau. We headed north and Kagbeni was soon out of sight behind us. The trail started out along the east side of the flat wide stony riverbed of the Kali Gandaki, at an altitude of about 9500 feet. It was a broad landscape, with snow peaks in the distance to the east, south, and west. Snowmelt runoff streams carved their way through rugged valleys to reach the Kali Gandaki. The valleys were mostly barren, covered with scree and scrub brush in hues of pale red, gray, yellow, and brown. Cliffs and ridges towered above us on both sides of the wide riverbed. The sunlight was intense, but we had some relief from the strong winds that swept down upon us, gusting from time to time, but never letting up.

Unlike the southern two-thirds of Nepal, there were no green paddy fields or trees here, only sand and rocks and some scrub bushes. At the end of the valley we could see a steep ridge rising high above the valley floor. We walked until we came to a little wooden bridge across a river that flowed into the Kali Gandaki. On the other side was a steep path traversing up a narrow and rock-lined canyon. We climbed up and up and up for over two hours when we were confronted with a pack train coming down this steep cliff path. There were about six mules and two Tibetan herders making their way south. The mules each had large rough tan wool pack bags filled with salt. The bags were swinging back and forth. There was almost no space on the path for both us and the mules, so we pressed ourselves into the ridge wall so that they could pass, without anyone getting pushed off the path.

Tony encounters pack burros with shorn wool on the trail between Kagbeni and Tangbe.

PART 2

On the Tibetan Plateau

September 29 (continued)

We kept climbing and finally got to the top of the ridge. We realized that the path did not go back down into a valley but stretched out horizontally in front of us through flat, bare and gently rolling hills, all at about 10-12,000 feet. At last, we had arrived on the Tibetan plateau.

It was hard to judge distance as we trekked north. The high altitude, the thin air, the bright sun, and the wild landscape all together seemed to change our perception, as we trekked on and on. Is all that we see and sense around us floating by us, or are we slowly moving through it? Where are we? Are we on the roof of the world? Where are we going? Many of these days felt like a wide-awake surreal dream.

We reached Tangbe about noon. It was a small village with some striking red and white chortens. We continued along the east side of the Kali Gandaki, through Chusang. It was marked as a town on our rudimentary map of Nepal, but there were only three houses set back from the trail, and they were all empty. On a ridge above us there was a large two-story building that might have been a lamasery. All the buildings were in disrepair. It looked as if the town had been abandoned. What happened? There was no one to ask.

Sometime about mid-afternoon we crossed over from the east side of the Kali Gandaki, over a small cantilevered bridge at Chele. The trail took us northwest towards Samar. It was a very steep climb up a cliff face. Steps were cut into the soft limestone. We were leaving the Kali Gandaki below, as the main trail to Lo Manthang took us high above the riverbed. On this steep and narrow cliff trail, we squeezed by women from nearby villages carrying baskets of yak dung and scrub juniper for fuel and compost. Even more challenging were the encounters with yak and dzo caravans. The northbound caravans often carried boxes of manufactured goods, like textiles. The southbound caravans often carried bulging wool sacks of salt from Tibet.

It was a long steep meandering trail through barren country to the town of Samar where we hoped to stay for the night. As we walked across low brown rolling hills, the land began to slope down slightly and we saw some green fields in the distance. Dark clouds were piled up against ridges behind the village. Daylight was fading fast, the temperature was dropping fast, and we were about to drop from fatigue.

As we approached, we could see familiar Tibetan-style houses bunched together with a narrow path

Women climbing up steps cut into sandstone, with dung-filled baskets, between Chusang and Chele.

between them. There were some children playing at the edge of the village and we stopped to ask if this was Samar. A few men and women appeared and seemed suspicious. We tried to explain that we were looking for the village headman. We used the Nepali term, "mukhiya" for headman. They shook their heads which confused us. Were they saying the headman was not there? Or where they telling us we should just go on our way and leave them alone? We went back and forth for a while, neither side understanding the other. David took out the letter of introduction and showed it to the growing number of villagers, pointing to the mukhiya's name that Amdo Kesang had written — in Tibetan — on the envelope. Nobody came forward to take it. We were reluctant to go any closer because there were Tibetan mastiff dogs chained nearby who were beginning to growl. David tossed the letter on the ground in front of the group. Someone grabbed it and went running back into the village. We waited for a while, and then a man arrived and welcomed us warmly into the town, much to our relief.

There was one more obstacle to overcome, the Tibetan mastiffs. We followed our host down the narrow village lane. Most houses had dogs on chains fastened to their doors. They snarled and lunged at us as we went by, but there was just enough space in the lane for us to walk carefully past the dogs as they strained at their chains, clawing the air trying to reach us. The children following us thought this was amusing. We didn't, but it was another memorable moment on our journey. When we arrived at the man's house, he pulled his dog aside and tied it up. We followed him inside. Finally and fortunately, we had found food and lodging for the night.

We entered a room where a few tall, young Tibetan men had been sitting. Behind them, leaning against the wall were several new rifles. They stood up, picked up their rifles and left, with little more than a nod at us. We smiled and nodded at them. They sure looked like Khampas to us. It was hard to guess what they thought of us. They just observed us with curiosity and did not try to ask us anything. We wondered where their camps were. What did they know about the border raids? We didn't ask. That really wasn't much of an option, because very few of them spoke any Nepali at all, and we didn't know much Tibetan.

We looked around the dimly lit room. It had red mud plastered walls and an adobe cook stove in the middle. An elderly woman spread straw mats for us, and then Tibetan carpets to sit on and rough woven pillows to lean against. We sat around the stove. The woman put brass tumblers in front of us which she filled with chang (Tibetan beer). Whenever we took a sip, she would refill the tumbler. We finally figured it out. If you don't want any more, do not drink a drop. It was a good meal with rice and dal, offered by a friendly family, all the more welcome after our initial misunderstandings.

After eating, as we were getting ready to sleep, we noticed there was a stack of rifles in the far corner of the room, with a bandolier of grenades hanging from a hook on the wall. They had been covered by the carpets and pillows. We slept fitfully, with lots of dreams, probably triggered by this strange, ominous, and wild place we found ourselves in. The altitude certainly added to our fatigue and restlessness.

Tony remembers dreaming of food, "a thick rare juicy steak." He remembers having visions of people

Approaching a wooden cantilevered bridge across the Kali Gandaki at the bottom of the gorge near Chele.

in his dreams talking to him seriously, but he couldn't remember what they said. "Maybe this was why prophets went into the desert and came out with visions and images and stories," Tony said. "Maybe the desert helped them to find something beyond themselves. It was as if my mind rebelled against the emptiness of the world we had walked through during the day and created these bright vivid images. If I had stayed longer maybe I would have learned to talk to the people in my dreams." The next morning, we did talk about our dreams, and wondered what they meant.

Not long before dawn, we heard the drone of a propeller plane heading north. Then — only 15 minutes later — it returned, heading south. Who was it? Where were they from? What were they doing? Air drops of supplies and weapons? Much later, we learned about CIA activities in the area, supporting the Khampas. But we never did find out for sure what that mystery prop plane was doing up there on its dawn flight.

David and Tony in lower right corner start climbing up a narrow and steep trail toward Samar.

David encounters pack mule with juniper brush on cliff trail to Samar.

Villagers with Juniper
brush, heading down
the cliff trail, to cross the
Ghyakar Khola, and then
to climb up to Samar and
Ghyakar villages on the
other side of the gorge.

Tony and David, now high above the river gorge, wondering about the trail ahead to Samar.

Surreal landscape of Ghyakar village, near Samar.

September 30

We got up and found ourselves still hungry after yesterday's exhausting trek. A young man by the name of Tarji cooked a delicious meal for us of rice, dal, and yak meat.

When we started this trek, we hadn't thought much about where to find food along the way, especially on the more remote and unfamiliar northern side of the Himalayas. We did have those letters of introduction from Amdo Kesang, but that would only provide for a few meals in a few places. But somehow, after we crossed the Himalayas, we were treated as guests almost everywhere we went. Rarely was payment ever requested or accepted.

We left Samar quite early. With our sketchy maps, we thought it would be a pretty long day. We had no idea just how things would go for food and evening shelter. We walked through bare rocky rolling hills made of gravel and rocks. It looked like it could have been the surface of the moon. There was just an occasional tuft of scrubby juniper growth. There was little sign of any human habitation.

The few encounters we did have on the trail were extraordinary, if not incredible. At one stage we saw a man coming towards us, barefoot, wearing rags and with long scraggly hair. We wondered where he was coming from and how he could have gotten here.

Fork in the trail. No signs. Which way to go? We took the high road to the left.

He just seemed to have come out of nowhere and suddenly appeared in front of us. As he approached, he gave us a traditional Nepali greeting of "Namaste" and asked us, "Nepal-ko halkhabar ke-ho?" "What's the news from Nepal?" He passed us and kept on walking.

Once, we came to the top of a small ridge, and looked down at several men chatting, laughing, and playing some gambling or card game at the bottom of a dry stream bed. We gave them a few smiles as we passed them. They paid little attention to us. We hiked up the trail to the next ridge and started down again. They were out of sight and we heard them no more. It felt like they must have been only apparitions, a hallucination triggered by this wild, empty landscape.

After about 4 hours, we saw the small village of Ghiling. Just ahead of us, a few Tibetans were approaching us on the trail. They had the now-familiar appearance of local traders or Khampas, with long black hair, high boots, colorful robes, and the usual daggers in decorated silver sheaths. They turned off to a house just by the trail, and we followed them in hopes of finding some food or drink. We had a little dried cheese, and 3 or 4 cups of Tibetan tea. We were finally getting used to the taste. It wasn't anything like any tea we were used to "back in Nepal." However, it was a very good energy boost, and a good way to prevent dehydration. The other Tibetans at this tea stop smiled, laughed, and chatted with each other, but not with us. They glanced at us now and then. What were they thinking about us? And what brought them to this place? By now, we were well aware that there was a lot going on around us we didn't understand. We wished we could communicate better with people we met along the way. We didn't even have a bilingual dictionary with us.

After leaving this midday tea stop, we headed north again. The landscape became even more forbidding and desolate, a moonscape in light browns and grays. As we climbed higher, the gusty winds blew fine dust across the pass we were approaching. We had reached Nyi-La Pass and surveyed the landscape. At about 13,000 feet or 4000 meters, this was the highest point on our journey, and the highest point on the trail from Nepal to Tibet. It was also the unofficial southern border entry to the old Kingdom of Mustang. But there was nobody up here but we three, mildly hallucinatory trekkers. The scenery was truly extraordinary, with expansive views of valleys rimmed by high ridges to the north, west, and east, and to the south were the giant mountain ranges of Dhaulagiri, Nilgiri and Annapurna. The vision remained as we descended from the pass. We finally made it into Ghemi about 4 P.M.

A number of friendly villagers came out to meet us here, with smiles and namastes. Our Tibetan friend in Pokhara, Amdo Kesang, had given us a letter to his friend in Ghemi, Amji Somdu. A few villagers led us to his house. When he came to the door he did not look very friendly or happy with our presence. His Nepali was very limited. David gave him the letter from Amdo Kesang, and that improved our reception immensely. He took us to a large room, rolled out five plush rugs, and gestured for us to sit. Over the next few hours we were served cups of Tibetan tea, then cups of spiced milk, then more than enough chang (Tibetan beer). He told us and showed us that he had a very painful tooth and gum infection. We gave him aspirin and told him that he should get down to Pokhara as soon as possible to have it taken care of.

Longest Mani prayer wall in Mustang District, on the trail into Ghemi.

More than a few times, people we met along the way asked us to give them medicine for various aches and pains and illness. It was often an awkward situation. We handed out aspirin here and there, trying to let them know it might not help that much. It occurred to us that Amji Somdu's attitude when we arrived probably had more to do with his painful infection than our presence.

The room where we were to sleep had thick and luxurious rugs. There were tangkas on the walls, along with bells of various sizes. A few different kinds of drums and horns and cymbals were scattered here and there. We thought this was a prayer room, but there was no puja or prayer in this room that night or in the morning. The room gave us a feeling of physical and spiritual protection. It felt warm and safe, a break from all the wind and dust and immense landscapes and vistas we had been trekking through. The warmth came also from drinking lots of tea and chang.

View from the pass of the trail into Ghemi.

Caravansery rest stop for yak and dzo.

October 1

We had a good breakfast meal of wheat bread, potatoes, and curd. Soon after leaving Ghemi, we came upon a very long Mani wall, made of carved stone tablets and slates. The carvings had mantras or devotional designs, as spiritual offerings. Many had the inscription "Om Mani Padme Hum." Originally a Sanskrit mantra, it has been translated in many ways by many Buddhist traditions. A simple metaphoric translation is "hail to the jewel in the lotus." We later found out this was the longest Mani wall in Mustang District measuring 1,003 feet in length.

After a few hours of walking through the dry, rocky moonscape, we climbed up to a pass to discover a junction in the trail. One path went northwest and seemed to go due west into the distance. The other went northeast through and then behind some more dry rocky hills. There were no markers and nothing to tell us which path would lead us to Lo Manthang. We wondered which path we should take, or whether we should wait until someone came who could give us some information. After waiting a while, and not seeing anyone anywhere, we finally took the high road to the left and continued trekking.

Later, as we walked around a hill we saw off in the distance a cloud of dust and then realized that it was a group of horsemen. They galloped towards us. Tony dropped down to one knee and starting filming them with his movie camera. As he raised the camera to his eye, he realized they all had rifles. His filming might look like someone with a gun pointing at them. He quickly stopped and put away his camera. We watched with growing alarm as they rode up to us — about 50 feet away — and checked us out. There were about 20 Khampas on small Tibetan horses, with the now-familiar dark dusty red robes and long sprawling strands of hair. They were well-armed with rifles and bandoliers of grenades. They looked us over and then turned and rode off leaving a cloud of dust. We breathed a sigh of relief and resumed our way north.

Further on, we saw someone riding on horseback on the far side of the river gorge, perhaps a half-mile away. As far as we could make out, he was wearing a bright blue, fiber or down-filled mountain parka, a very unusual outfit for local inhabitants. Perhaps it was a Chinese scout out for a trail ride.

On the approach to Tsarang, we passed through an especially large and magnificent chorten gate just outside the town. As we walked through the village, looking for food and lodging, we were greeted and welcomed by Lobsom, son-in-law of the King of Mustang. Even though he spoke no Nepali, we understood that he was offering his home for food and lodging. His wife, the daughter of the King, gave us tea. We sipped the tea and rested our weary feet.

Afterwards, we asked if we could visit the large gompa of Tsarang. Lobsom immediately took us there. It was a remarkable place, part of a large monastery complex that once housed hundreds of monks of the Gelup sect. Here we met the head lama of Tsarang, Jigme Lama. We learned he was the eldest son of the King of Mustang. Jigme Lama stopped his prayers to greet us in his room of worship. Jigme did not speak

Women spreading grain stalks for threshing, near Tsarang.

Threshing the grain with hinged wooden flails.

David and Tony, on top of Lobsom's house, son-in-law of the King. Tsarang Gompa in the background.

Nepali, but someone there translated for us. It was a brief but friendly exchange before he resumed his prayers. We thanked him for meeting us and told him Tsarang was a lovely town and that its gompa was magnificent. His worship room and a few others adjacent to it were filled with tongkas, golden statues of Buddha, incense, horns, bells, and prayer books. These Tibetan scriptures were wooden-covered and cloth-bound stacks of manuscript sheets.

When we returned to Lobsom's house for the night, a young boy was sent along with us. It was getting late and a number of homes had guard dogs chained outside the entrance to their houses. But they stretched those chains to growl at us. The boy threw stones at the dogs to keep them from getting too close to us. He seemed at least as scared as we were. All we needed was a deep dog bite in the leg. How could we limp back to "Nepal?" What about rabies? There would be no medical evacuation up here.

We managed to make it back safely to Lobsom's house without having any of those mastiffs sink its teeth into us. We had a decent meal of wheat bread, potatoes, goat meat, and tea. Many people up here subsist mostly on tsampa (barley or wheat flour) mixed with tea or water. We were lucky to get as much food as we did. Some days we weren't so lucky.

Lobsom's wife, the daughter of the King, was hard to figure out. At times, she seemed grumpy and withdrawn as we waited for food. Perhaps the princess was not too happy with her life in this humble household. Perhaps we were an unwelcome distraction from other concerns she had. We would never know. She chain-smoked, drawing cigarettes from an engraved gold cigarette case. She lit them with a silver lighter studded with tiny jewels. After dinner, she started up a kind of gambling game with her husband and two other men. Her spirits picked up considerably during the game. Some kind of coins that were not Nepali were pushed out and pulled back as games were won and lost. High stakes? Who knows, they all seemed to be having a great time no matter where the coins ended up. We finally finished off the night with some chang and soon were fast asleep.

View of the interior courtyard of Lobsom's house. Note ladder carved out of a log in the foreground. Chorten memorial on the right. Large house of the royal family on the left.

October 2

We left Tsarang about mid-morning after a meager meal of wheat bread with Tibetan tea. We were really missing that good old dal-bhat. Not surprisingly, we were often tired. The terrain around our route was desolate, with no sign of growth or green or life. Suddenly, as we came up from a low dip in the trail, we saw about 500 yards ahead of us a pack train of yak and horses, with several Khampas carrying highly-polished rifles in the morning sun. They stopped when they saw us, fiddled with the packs on the animals, and then moved off the trail a bit to let us pass. We exchanged a few nods and smiles. Our conversation would have been awkward. They were clearly carrying weapons and ammunition for their guerrilla war against the Chinese. What did they think we were doing there? Admiring the scenery?

Passing a yak and dzo pack train with shorn wool and woven wool sacks, possibly with salt.

Rest break for fuel gatherers.

PART 3

Lo Manthang

October 2 (continued)

After a long slow uphill stretch, we reached Lo La Pass at the crest of a ridge. There we got the first view of our journey's destination, the walled city of Lo Manthang. We all stopped and stared, speechless at this astounding sight. The town was nestled in a fairly large round basin, surrounded by a ring of ridgelines. The northern arc of the ring — from 4 to 8 miles away — was the border separating Mustang and Nepal from Tibet and China. There were about 5 hamlets scattered around Lo Manthang. Around each were bright green and yellow cultivated fields of wheat, barley, root crops, mustard seed, and potatoes. As we approached the fields, we saw women swinging scythes and beating sheaves of grain with hinged, wooden flails. The tops of red and white gompas could be seen within the city and scattered elsewhere around the valley. There were two buildings on two steep hills to the northeast and northwest of Lo Manthang. We later found them on maps as features named Nyamdo and San Dzong. One of them appeared to be a siege fortress. The other might have been one of the King's residences.

From the pass, we could see two of the high thick walls of the city, but no gate or entrance. How do we get inside the walls of Lo Manthang? Where was the check-post? We had been expecting some military or police presence before we arrived at the town itself. We walked slowly ahead, the trail sloped slightly downhill. Oddly, there was not a person in sight. In fact, we hardly ever saw any able-bodied men in or around the town. Curiouser and curiouser. We walked around to the third wall of the town. Still no gate or entrance of any kind. We finally turned the corner after the third wall and found the one and only entrance to the city, a wide and tall gateway framed by square posts and topped by a wide flat lintel.

Near the entrance gate, there were a few people. A couple of them just stared, some smiled, and a few said something to us — or about us. Someone quickly came up to us and said he was Amdo Kesang's friend and was expecting our arrival. We told him that we had a letter from the son of the King of Mustang and showed him the letter. He took us directly to his house. We later learned it was the house of Ghimerujhum, the town headman or chief, (mukhiya in Nepali). Our host seemed to be an agreeable person. He himself was related to the royal family, although we weren't exactly sure how. We met his wife — perhaps a princess — as well as some relatives. One of them was apparently another son of the King of Mustang, and had been appointed a Captain in the Nepali Army. We had a letter from Lobsom (the son-in-law of the King, whose house we stayed in at Tsarang) introducing us to this Captain. Our new acquaintances didn't know quite what to make of us, even with the letter from Lobsom. How much credibility did we have as trekkng tourists in the midst of all these border skirmishes and Khampa camps scattered around Mustang?

We walked along a cobble-stone street off to the left of the city gates and for a short way until we came to a door with carved lintel and paneling. We went up to the flat roof of the house. It was like many others throughout Mustang, with wood stacked around the perimeter and dung drying in places here and there. The view, however, was astonishing. Within the walls of the city were temples, gompas, large sturdy houses, with tall prayer flags flying from the top of many of them. Beyond the walls were a few settlements encircled by cultivated fields, and beyond them were small look-out guard posts and forts.

After taking in the remarkable rooftop view, we went back down inside. The room where we were to stay and sleep was quite nice. Tibetan rugs were spread around most of the floor. There were a few low tables for food and tea. At one end of the room a rack of mailbox type shelves and slots were filled with oblong prayer books and scriptures. On shelves and cupboards around the room, we saw Buddha images, tongkas, and oil lamps. The kitchen area was next door. The room was about 20 by 20 feet square. Over the hearth was a 2 by 2 foot opening in the ceiling, with a wooden cover for the vent. It had a good draft to pull most of the smoke out of the room, unlike so many cooking areas in Nepali homes. We put our packs in the front of the room against the wall, and sat down to rest and wait for tea and momo.

The door opened and a Nepali Army Subedar (officer) came in, with a few soldiers, all in uniform. He asked us what we were doing there and asked us for our travel pass. We said our passports were in our packs and went to get them out. He shook his head and said that what he meant was our Nepal government travel pass to visit Mustang. That's the moment we had the sinking realization that our visit to Lo Manthang was not going to be what we had hoped for. We explained that we had been invited to visit the King of Mustang by his son. We showed him our letter of introduction from Amdo Kesang. He didn't seem impressed. We said we hoped to see the town and visit the gompas. We told him we didn't want to cause any problems. If we could not stay, we would leave. He said that this would not be possible now and that he would need to find out from Kathmandu what to do with us. Until he had instructions, we would have to stay in this house.

It turned out there was indeed a checkpoint, but it was within the walls of Lo Manthang. We thought that it would be somewhere along the trail outside the town. The Subedar told us — with some embarrassment — that we were not supposed to be here in the first place. Major Rana in Jomsom had wired the Subedar instructions. If we showed up in this area or Lo Manthang itself, we were to be detained. Then he had to wire army headquarters in Kathmandu for further instructions. So we found ourselves under some kind of house arrest.

It was a modestly congenial detention under the circumstances. We were not to leave the home of our host, Ghimerujhum. The Subedar was quite apologetic. He was sure this situation would be cleared up quickly.

Stu at Lo La Pass. Lo Manthang is in the center background.

Approaching Lo Manthang. Note siege fort and royal refuge on the hilltops beyond the town.

We weren't so sure about that. What did it mean to "clear it up?" How long would it take? Almost all government agencies were closed for the long Desain holiday. What were we able to do in the meantime? How much freedom did we have to explore the town? Could we contact the King of Mustang? What would happen when the Peace Corps found out about our predicament? What could we do about our declining health? The exhausting trek, the scarcity of food, and our intestinal cramps and runs were all taking a physical toll. It didn't help that at this high altitude and thin air pressure, we couldn't boil water hot enough to sterilize anything.

We asked if we could send a message to the U.S. embassy in Kathmandu. He agreed to let us write something that would be sent through the Nepal Army wireless radio system. We got together and thought for a few minutes and then wrote a note: "Help. We are being detained in Mustang. Please expedite our release. Profound regrets, Stu, Tony, David." The Subedar said our message would be sent the next day.

We asked the Subedar to supply us with some rice. He agreed to send some over to us from the barracks. Without much protein, rice, or vegetables, we had been getting weaker and having more stomach problems. We saw what the farm workers ate and wondered how they managed. They worked in Ghimerujhum's fields and came in for a simple midday meal of tsampa mixed by hand with warm water. It was hard to see how they lived on just this.

We got our packs and were led to a room down the hallway from the reception room and a Nepali guard was stationed at the door. We spread our sleeping bags and got ready to stay for a while. We couldn't leave the room without an escort, so we laid out our sleeping bags in one corner of the room and designated the other corner for our latrine.

A spry old woman in this household served us Tibetan tea with a toothless smile. After a while, she beckoned us into the main room where she had prepared some rice and dhal, provided by the Nepal Army officer. But the dhal was full of stones and the rice was stale or mildewed. We all got sick to the stomach, literally. To make things even worse, we were kept in this one room, so we had to use the latrine corner to relieve ourselves. It was a dreadful night of sporadic spasms of gas and diarrhea.

October 3

The guard took us up to the roof where we could sit in the sun and see the other rooftops in the city. We played cards and read and talked and thought about whether and when we would hear from the Embassy and whether we would be released and what would happen.

Three Nepali Army privates were assigned to keep an eye on us, one each in 8 hour shifts. Eventually, we were able to go out to walk around a few nearby houses between our place and the army barracks. The Nepali soldiers were nice to us, but they complained about the rough conditions up here so far from the "real" Nepal south of the Himalayas.

We met two Indian radio operators who had been

53

On top of Ghimeruzhum's house, grandma stands amid fuel wood and dung. As matron of the house, she carried the keys. In the background, the main gompa, many chortens, hill top retreats.

reassigned from Darjeeling and Assam to help monitor conditions along the Mustang border. They were dreading the coming winter, when snow can pile up to 4 feet deep. They too missed good, home-cooked food.

We did manage to buy a large quantity of potatoes. At night we sat around the fire with some of the family. David played the harmonica. We sang a few songs.

October 4

Our message had been sent to Kathmandu, but as of midday there was no response from the U.S. Embassy or from anyone in the Nepal government or army. We wandered over to the barracks, with one of our Nepali army acquaintances, and had tea with the Subedar. We asked about getting more rice because we were still hungry.

After dinner, Stu discovered that 250 Rupees, his back-up pair of glasses, and his passport were missing from his Kelty backpack. What happened? Who took the stuff? Was it one of the field workers or soldiers? Why would they take Stu's passport? How long had it been missing? We doubted that anyone in the household family would steal anything. David and Tony checked their stuff and found nothing missing. We wondered where that money and passport would ultimately end up.

David, on the roof of our detention house. It did have some scenic consolations.

We found out much later on. Harry Barnes, the US Deputy Chief of Mission, and a good friend of ours from Peace Corps training, told us afterwards that he had received our message. But the geographic name of Mustang had been replaced, apparently for security reasons. It now said "Help. We are being detained in a cave. Please expedite our release. Profound regrets, Stu, Tony, David." Harry didn't know what to make of that. But very soon afterwards, the CIA sent an urgent cable from Washington to Kathmandu inquiring about these wayward PCVs. Radio Beijing broadcast a story that Stuart Ullmann (by name) and other CIA agents were fomenting trouble on their border with Nepal. That report also made its way to Washington and then to Kathmandu.

David, writing notes. Young girl watches. Indian border guard keeps us company.

We had a picnic outing by this stream, with our "guardians," as a herd of goats grazed by us.

October 5

Ghimerujhum was still out of town, so we found his older brother and told him about the theft. He said he would try to find out what he could about the theft. We all agreed not to tell any of the Indian or Nepali army staff about the thefts. That might create a larger problem and delay our departure. More bad news: for the third day in a row, we were still all suffering from diarrhea. Our potato supply ran out. We were getting weaker every day.

With two of our Nepali guards with us, we were allowed to go outside the city walls on a "picnic." The Nepalis were glad to be with us, something to do for them. They hated being posted here. The food was lousy and they missed "Nepal." Our picnic consisted of a couple of packets of biscuits we were able to buy, and some fizzies dropped in a canteen. We lay in the sun, washed our socks in a small stream, and took turns heading off behind boulders to relieve ourselves. Just before we left to go back, a hawk swooped down and picked off Stu's only bar of soap from a rock. What a lousy day.

First photo after our release, we are heading south toward Tsarang and the Nilgiri Mountains.

October 6

The Indian radio operator and the Nepali Subedar came over about 10 A.M. with good news. Kathmandu authorities had given orders for our release, with instructions to return to Pokhara directly. We decided we would leave immediately. We stuffed our sleeping bags and our clothes into our packs. An army private took us to the city gates and we left. Ghimerujhum was still out of town, but we left on good terms with the rest of his family. We also exchanged farewells with the army personnel. Ghimerujhum's older brother said he would keep trying to find out about Stu's money, glasses, and passport. At this point, Stu couldn't care less.

We were just glad to be released and ready to hit the trail. Well, we weren't really ready. We were out of shape for trekking and still weak. But we walked fast anyway. We had a lot of ground to cover and we were anxious about our fate as PCVs. We rushed past Tsarang, and reached Ghemi just before dark, exhausted. Amji Somdi was out of town, but his son and daughter were there. They made dinner for us, along with lots of Tibetan tea. It tasted good, a restorative for body and soul.

Goat-herder in front of his tent.

David taking a break. The Annapurnas are in the background, to the south.

October 7

We had a good breakfast of rice, potato, and radish. It was a long tough day on the trail. We still had bouts of diarrhea, gas, and fatigue. We didn't go through any villages, and only saw a few houses off the trail. We trekked nearly seven hours that day. Our main consolation was an extraordinary view of the northern side of the Annapurna Range. We limped into Samar at 4 P.M., exhausted. We again encountered snarling dogs chained near the entrance of our lodging. Fortunately, we got around them, and into the house. None of us wanted to go out to relieve ourselves and risk any encounter with those dogs. If you had to go, go up on the roof.

Thakali women doing the laundry in Marpha.

October 8

Samar to Jomsom, another long hard exhausting day. We were moving fast, heading south at about twice the pace as we had headed north. We didn't meet Major Rana, and didn't want to. Tony picked up some stuff he had stashed at Kagbeni.

October 9

Feeling very weak, it took us a while to get from Jomsom to Tukche. On the way, at Marpha, we met another Peace Corps Volunteer from our group, Don Messerschmidt. He gave us some bad news. Word was getting around that we three, and maybe our whole Peace Corps group in Nepal, were in real trouble because of our unauthorized Mustang trek. When we got to Tukche we met some more Peace Corps Volunteers from our group, Phil Brandt, Stu During, and Bruce Morrison. They were mountain climbing in the area, but got delayed by a missing porter. The six of us all stayed at the same place, and shared good food and drink. We had chang, more chang, and then still more chang. It was a good night to get soused, forget about stomach problems, exhaustion, and any penalties we might incur for our Mustang trek.

October 10

Tukche to Ghasa, onward and downward we cruised.

October 11

We took a short-cut on the way back home, but it involved a lot more ups and downs. Our route went from Ghasa to Dana to Tatopani to Sikha. We stayed at a Magar place in Sikha.

October 12

We climbed from Sikha to Gorepani, a 3-hour steep ascent and even steeper descent through thick forest. Near Gorepani, we reached the ridgeline, with its spectacular views of Dhaulagiri, Tukche Peak, and Annapurnas. David's knee and leg were really hurting. He hired a porter to carry his pack. We arrived in Biratanti just at dark, and stayed in a marvelous Thakali house. It seemed incredible to us. It had a staircase with banister handrails, chairs, tables, mattresses, great food, and raksi. Glory hallelujah.

Domesticated Tibetan goats, on the trail, between Geling and Samar.

Dhaulagiri and Tukche mountain peaks, near Sikha.

October 13

After an early start, and a few hours on the trail, we got to Lumle, the first village back in Kaski District. After another two hours, Hyangja came into view. We were almost home. This would be the last day of our trek, but not the last day of our adventures. And misadventures.

We parted ways outside of Hyangja. David and his porter went off in search of medical treatment for his swollen left knee joint at the Shining Hospital near Pokhara, the only hospital in the district. There wasn't much they could do, except ease the swelling and pain. No more trekking for David for a while. But they did have a short-wave radio. The Peace Corps arranged a helicopter evacuation for David to Kathmandu the next day.

That night, two Khampas also arrived at the hospital. One of them was wounded and was seeking medical help. David inquired with the Nepali thumb-and-forefinger gesture "Ke garne?" What happened? He got a finger-gun gesture reply. He had been shot and wounded.

When Tony and Stu reached Pokhara, they were met by our Peace Corps Director, Willi Unsoeld. He berated us for the stupidity of our escapade. He told us how we had almost caused an international incident and almost gotten the Peace Corps thrown out of Nepal.

Several Nepali government and US Embassy personnel were quite angry with us and wanted us to be terminated and expelled from the country. But government offices were all closed during the long Desain holiday. No officials were in the foreign ministry to deal with the incident. No decisions could be taken.

One immediate decision was made for David to undergo surgery at Shanta Bhawan Hospital in Kathmandu to repair a stress fracture and splintering of his tibia. A few days later, Harry Barnes guided David, with cast and crutches, into a Nepal foreign ministry office to make suitable apologies for our wayward actions.

Harry and Willi tactfully suggested that this incident would best be dealt with as an internal matter of Peace Corps – Nepal. Our pay was docked for the month. All our remaining leave was cancelled. Hobbled by his injury, David was transferred to Kathmandu for the rest of his service.

Willi asked how we felt about what we had done. We told him how sorry we were for all the trouble we caused. He agreed that we had certainly caused a great deal of trouble and almost caused an international incident. But if he had been in our shoes and had the opportunity to go to Mustang, he would have done the same thing.

EPILOGUE

Our trek to the ancient walled town of Mustang took 24 days. It took us 12 days to get there, 4 nights within its wall, and 8 days to return to Pokhara. Our story has ended but it raised issues that are still unresolved.

We never did meet the King of Mustang — Angun Tenzing Trandul — on our trek. But we did meet his eldest son and successor — Jigme Dorje Trandul — when he was the head lama at Tsarang. He became King when his father died later in 1964. In 2008, after several major constitutional changes, King Jigme Dorje Palbar Bista lost his royal status by an act of the Nepali parliament. He was the 25th and last King in a direct line of hereditary rulers dating back to 1380. Although he no longer has the title of King or Raja or Gyelpo, his sovereignty endures widely in Mustang.

When we started our trek, we knew little about the Khampas in Mustang. They were anti-Chinese resistance fighters from the eastern Tibetan region of Kham. They had first taken up arms against the Chinese PLA in the 1950's. By 1960, they had set up a base camp for their covert guerrilla operations in the Mustang district. They received supplies and training from the CIA and reportedly from the Kuomintang government in Taiwan. Some were even sent to military training camps in the Colorado Rockies. However, American support was limited. It ended in the early 1970's after Secretary of State Henry Kissinger started secret negotiations to establish diplomatic relations between the U.S. and China. A lot is now known about these "orphans of the Cold War." For more information, search online for the "CIA Tibetan Program."

The governments of Nepal and China exchanged embassies and signed boundary settlement agreements in the 1960's. More recently, China has been steadily increasing aid, trade, and infrastructure investment in the region. Some local monasteries have been restored and new ones have been built with Chinese funds. A new road linking Mustang to Tibet in the north and Nepal to the south will likely transform the former kingdom. Local shops are now filled with Chinese groceries and supplies. Chinese officials and Chinese tourists are now regular visitors. China has found the "lost kingdom."

Looking south at the terraced fields of Samar and Ghyakar, then the Nilgiri and Annapurna ranges.

What are the current prospects for the Tibetan refugees and communities we encountered on our journey? Many have moved on to other places in Nepal, India, and even Australia. Those who remained soon moved beyond their impoverished refugee conditions with considerable help of food, clothing, shelter and other aid. The original Tashi Palkhiel Tibetan settlement near Pokhara now includes a public school — the Mt. Kailash School with over 200 students through grade 7 — a combined kindergarten/nursery/day care center, a Tibetan Buddhist religious school, a monastery, a health clinic, a handicraft cooperative, and a carpet trading company. It has many tourist visitors, a volunteer internship program, and a website. Several other Tibetan groups have also settled in the area. In sum, it is a thriving community.

What will happen to the next generation of Tibetans in Nepal? Would they return to Tibet if it became possible? What will happen after the 14th Dalai Lama? There are many uncertainties ahead. Like the ancient Israelites after the destruction of the Holy Temples in Jerusalem, there may be a significant Tibetan diaspora for many generations to come. They will have many challenges in maintaining their cultural identity in exile and in maintaining ties with their "homeland."

How did this trek affect us personally? How did it influence our choices and attitudes over the course of our lives? We had a truly awe-inspiring experience travelling through the Himalayas. We were awed by the natural geological cathedral we went through. We were fascinated by the ways people had adapted their lives to survive in a challenging physical environment, while at the same time preserving a deep religious tradition. However, to paraphrase the Prologue to this story, we also missed the full meaning of the social and political changes going on around us. We have written this story in our attempts to understand "something that is probably quite ineffable," how that experience has motivated our journey through life. For my own part, I still remember, cherish, and seek that sense of awe. As Abraham Joshua Heschel once said, "wonder rather than doubt is the root of all knowledge."

THEN AND NOW

Among the most enduring legacies of our Mustang trek and our Peace Corps service are the personal connections and affection we have for each other and for Nepal.

Tony Drexler

David Rosenberg

Stu Ullmann

Made in the USA
Charleston, SC
01 October 2016